Rules at Sc

by Katherine Scraper

I need to know these words.

read

rules

Rules at School
1. We do our work.
2. We put up our hand in class.
3. We walk in the hall.
4. We get in line.
5. We read books to learn.

school

teacher

We have rules at school.

We do our work.

We give our work
to the teacher.

Then we get time to play.

We put up our hand in class.
Then we can talk.

We walk in the hall.

We do not run.

Then we are safe.

We get in line.

We do not talk.

Then we can go outside to play.

We read every day.
We read books to learn.

We need rules.

Rules at School

1. We do our work.
2. We put up our hand in class.
3. We walk in the hall.
4. We get in line.
5. We read books to learn.